Translations Addenda

Other books by the same author include

MY GOD, YOU HAVE A LOT TO ANSWER
FOR, BUT YOU WON'T, WILL YOU
BOOK PARADISE: SPILLIKINS
LIKE THOSE OF AN EERIE RUIN
THE MAKING OF A STORY
LITHOS
collected to 2012 POEMS &
TRANSLATIONS *collected to 2012*
ANTONYMS ANEW: BARBS & LOVES
INEXPERIENCE AND UNCOMMON SENSE IN TRANSLATION
OSIP MANDELSTAM: WHOEVER HAS FOUND A HORSESHOE

LISTENING FOR HENRY CROWDER
UNNATURAL MUSIC
DESERT SANDS: STUFF SMITH
PURE AT HEART: STUFF SMITH
BLACK GYPSY: EDDIE SOUTH
FALLEN FROM THE MOON: JUICE WILSON
POEM ABOUT MUSIC

SNOW LIT REV, ED.

Anthony Barnett

TRANSLATIONS
- addenda -
originally printed in *Snow lit rev*

Dagerman Ekelöf Giroux
Glissant Molodowsky Pavese
Royet-Journoud Segalen
Supervielle Ungaretti Zanzotto

& an essay on Leopardi's The Infinite

A·B

Translations Addenda
Originally Printed in Snow lit rev
Copyright © Anthony Barnett 2023

Anthony Barnett is hereby identified as
the moral rights translator and where
applicable author of this work

All rights reserved

reprinting or online posting or scanning for
that purpose in whole or in part without
the written permission of the copyright
holder is prohibited except as allowed
in fair use in such as a review

Typeset in Centaur MT with one
glyph in after-Centaur Coelacanth
by AB©omposer

Printed by TJ Books Padstow

First published 2023 by
Allardyce Book ABP
14 Mount Street · Lewes · East Sussex BN7 1HL UK
www.abar.net

Distributed in USA by SPD
1341 Seventh Street · Berkeley CA 94710-1409
www.spdbooks.org

CIP records for this book are available from
The British Library and The Library of Congress

ISBN 978-0-907954-70-5

NOTE

Gathered here are all the translations I have finished since collected *Translations* (2012). All but one have appeared in the review *Snow lit rev*. Also included is an updated version of "Leopardi and The Infinite", which first appeared in a book of essays *Antonyms Anew: Barbs & Loves* (2016). Interested readers are directed to that book for other essays touching on translations, including Eileen Chang, Isak Dinesen, Gunnar Ekelöf, Clarice Lispector, Umberto Saba, Victor Segalen, César Vallejo, Andrea Zanzotto; and to the pamphlet of a 2003 Meiji University lecture *InExperience and UnCommon Sense in Translation* (2014). Also relevant is a 1992 conversation with D. S. Marriott, available on request. Osip Mandelstam, *Whoever Has Found a Horseshoe* (2023), published on the centenary of the original's first appearance in a Moscow review, is a further revision of four earlier versions (the third of which appeared in *Translations*) in light of new understanding and the latest established Russian text, which takes account of Mandelstam's own revisions.

A few reviews of translations have appeared in *PN Review*: Paul Celan, Nelly Sachs, a.o., search at https://www.pnreview.co.uk/ And one on Benjamin Fondane is posted at https://tearsinthefence.com/2018/01/15/benjamin-fondanes-cinepoems-and-others-and-existential-monday-new-york-review-books/

There are no revisions here to the first printings in *Snow lit rev*, except for corrections to a few small typos. *Snow lit rev* includes many prose and poetry translations by others, described at http://www.abar.net/snow.pdf/

The last page here has details about a translation roundtable held at Université de Lille on 12 December 2022.

Assistance has been gratefully received from Xavier Kalck (all French); Ian Brinton (Supervielle); Pauline Manière (Segalen); Barry Schwabsky, Tim Harris (Pavese); Jørn H. Sværen (Ekelöf); Éric Pesty, Claude Royet-Journoud, Ian Brinton (Giroux); Lo Dagerman (Dagerman); Vincent Moleta, Matilde Manara (Leopardi); Raphael Koenig (Molodowsky, which was an invitation).

AB, February 2023

ADDENDA TO

TRANSLATIONS

Akutagawa Albiach Delahaye Des Forêts
Giroux Lagerkvist Vesaas Zanzotto &
Berg Bernhard Celan Mandelstam Ungaretti

TRANSLATIONS

2012

Jules Supervielle *11*

Giuseppi Ungaretti *20*

Édouard Glissant *25*

Gunnar Ekelöf *31*

Claude Royet-Journoud *41*

Andrea Zanzotto *45*

Victor Segalen *48*

Cesare Pavese *54*

Roger Giroux *62*

Stig Dagerman *79*

"Giacomo Leopardi and The Infinite" *86*

appendices

Kadia Molodowsky *92*

"Rafael Alberti" *93*

JULES SUPERVIELLE

translated from the French

Five Poems

in Snow 7, Spring 2019

«Prophétie», «À une enfant»
in *Gravitations*, Gallimard, Paris, 1925

«Les Mains photographiées» of
which there appear to be two versions
the one here having additional lines
«Le Poids d'une journée»
in *Les Amis inconnus*, Gallimard, Paris, 1934

«Tu disparais»
in *1939–1945*, Gallimard, Paris, 1946

«Elle lève les yeux . . .»
in *Naissances*, Gallimard, Paris, 1951

Prophecy

to Jean Cassou

One day the Earth will be
Nothing but a blind space turning,
Confounding night and day.
Under the immense sky of the Andes
There will no longer be any mountains,
Not even a small ravine.

Of all the lodges in the world
Only a balcony won't dislodge
And of the human mappemonde
An overarching heartache.
Of the late Atlantic Ocean
A little salt taste in the air,
A flying and magical fish
That knows nothing of the sea.

In a nineteen-o-five coupé
(Four wheels and no road!)
Three girly girls of that epoque
Figures of vaporous apparition
Will peer out of the car door
Thinking that Paris can't be far
To catch only the odour
Of a sky that gags the throat.

Where there was a forest
A birdsong will soar
Which no one can place,
Prefer, or even hear,
But God, himself, all ears
He'll say: "It's a thistle finch."

To a Little Girl

Let your voice through the doors and the walls
Find me at length in my room, obscured by poetry,
O child who are my child,
You who display the wonderment of a garden trug posy by posy
        bundled with flowers, grasses, sweet-smelling herbs
When it thought it was forgotten in a corner,
And you turn toward me like a signpost in the forest marking out
        the paths.
The paint is faint,
One mixes up the distances
But one is reassured.

O deprivation!
You are not even sure that you own your own little frock or your bare
 feet in their sandals
Or that your eyes are really yours, let alone their wonder,
Or this plump mouth, or these keep mum words,
Do you even have the right to look from top to bottom at these trees
 that act as a barrier to the garden sky
With that many pine cones and teeming needles?
The sky is so wide that maybe there isn't a place beneath for a child
 as little as you,
Too much space can suffocate us just as much as if we did not have
 enough.
And yet you must, like grown people,
Brave the universe in full with its muffled movement;
Even the ants accommodate it ants' little ones too.
How will you cope with the horse-and-carriages on the roads, at
 their different speeds,
And the boilers of the ships that ship their fires out to sea?
Your eyes would find in mine the security you can draw upon
In this tall what's-its-name with its deep voice named a father in the
 houses,
If to throw a clear gaze upon the world is not enough.

Photographed Hands

Now they were entering a world of smooth surfaces,
Where even rocky mountains are soft, easy to the touch,
And held in the palm of the hand.
They were treated like a face for the first time in their lives,
And under the glare of arc lamps
They sensed the outline of a brow
And the first symptoms of a nascent physiognomy.
From far away memory was moving towards these virgin shores
With the calm of a swell that takes its time to form itself.
Knowledge in the brain was communicating at last with the thumb.
The thumb lightly acquiesced in its domain,
And while the exposure lasted
The hands gave their name to the sun, to a lovely day.
They called it "trembling" this slight hesitation
That came to them from the human heart, at the other end of their
      warm veins,
They understood that life is a passing, fragile thing.
Then, arc lamps rolled away,
They remembered nothing of what they had thought they had made out
Tongue-tied by such a short discussion with these luminous forces.
The moment had arrived when one could no longer,
Call them forgetful.

The Burden of a Single Day

Solitude, you enter my very own room armed with a host of beings:
It rains on the coat of this one, it snows on that one and this other one
    is lit by the July sun.
They arrive from all over, "Listen to me! Listen to me!"
Each one wanting to say a little more than the other.
There are those who look for a lost brother, others, their mistress,
    their children.
"I can't do anything for you."
They all want to get a word in before they disappear:
"Listen to me, then afterwards I'll leave straightaway, really."
They sign to me to sit down so they can go on talking.
"But I've told you I can't do anything for you,
Phantoms for my eyes and my ears!"
One stranger asks my forgiveness and disappears without telling me
    what crime it is he's committed,
There's a young girl who has crossed woods in a country far from ours,
An old woman who asks my advice: "Advice about what?"
She won't add another word and goes off in a huff.

Now the only things in the room are my quite long table, my books,
    my papers.
My lamp lights upon a head, and human hands,
My lips begin to dream on their own account as if they were orphans.

Disappearing

You are disappearing, already banked in brume
One rows towards you as if across the twilight,
You are alone among the years consuming you
In your arms the slimness of your last hopes and dreams.

Wherever you place your foot dead leaves have fallen
With the fading murmuration of former loves,
The moon shadowing you saps the last of your strength
You turn infinitely blue for your final day.

Yet one is wise to your despondent innocence
The little that is left you making your heart beat
Now and then a start lifts you and illumines you
Awakening in your night the splendours of owls.

She lifts her eyes ...

She lifts her eyes and the breeze is stilled,
She lowers her eyes, the countryside unrolls,
She turns her head a single rose is
Captured and so it also turns its head
And however far you look nothing is the same.

A Note About Translating Jules Supervielle

Readers of *Snow lit rev* will know that editorials and the like are not often to our liking. Unusually, then, I feel moved to write a little about translating Jules Supervielle, a poet who seems to restore one's humanity at moments when it might be in danger of being lost. French poems are not the easiest of poems to translate. Why should they be? Let us recall that Yves Bonnefoy said that the poem is nothing, that it is the poetry that is there to translate (though that is no carte blanche). For more than fifty years I have tried to translate Supervielle's poetry, turning to it now and then, only usually to abandon it. Early affection for his story "The Child of the Open Sea" did, however, come out in the title of my book *Poems for the Daughter of Charles Lievens*, as well as in one of its poems. Two *Snow* events have conspired—inspired—to renew translation efforts: Ian Brinton's translation of Philippe Jaccottet's piece[1]—which includes quotations from the poetry—which we felt needed a complement; and Lucy Rose Cunningham's poems which mention the Andes.[2] Supervielle also has a poem here mentioning the Andes, one of the earliest whose poetry I have tried over and over to translate, though Supervielle's is, so to speak, from a Uruguayan perspective, which of course is on the wrong side of the continent, while Cunningham's poems are from a Chilean perspective. So, with the assistance of Xavier Kalck, who has straightened out some points that clearly (or hazily) have troubled not only myself but also some other translators of Supervielle, I am happy to print, for the moment, these few. It is, though, proper to acknowledge that the felicitous title "The Burden of a Single Day" for «Le Poids d'une journée» is also found in an earlier translation, in *Selected Writings*, New Directions, 1967. It may not have come to me otherwise.

---

[1] "At the Heart of Supervielle"
[2] "Blue Is a Quiet"

GIUSEPPI UNGARETTI

translated from the Italien

Opening

Paris–Milan 1919

in Snow 2, Fall 2012–Spring 2013

Complete closing section of *L'Allegria*
Mondadori, Milan, 1942
entitled "Prime"

Return

Things ruffle a vast monotony of absence

Now a pale shell

The dark blue of the deep crushed

Now a stone mantle

An African in Paris

Whoever cross migrated from sun-beaten tracks where the women hide their fecund flesh and every screech reaches calmly like a memory,
Whoever from the exultation of seas submerged in skies descends into this city, discovers a clouded land and a savage soot.
Space is finite.
Am I no longer to be allowed an unprejudiced alarm nor under that sun that sparked and enjoined happy things, enchanting sojourns?
The temperamental man met a moment ago, lost among the countless streets must worry at turned amazements in the fatuous glares that surround him and at each and every moment the only thing his soul recalls is ridicule, and the wounds of his impatience.
He shall no longer be, unnaturally, afraid of death, but with no means of escape chosen as prey by the unremitting terror of the future, he will nevertheless delude himself in the belief that one unsuspected day he may reconcile the eternal if only through some tiresome scruple, predicted in the shortness of his breath, yearning that his mind may yet every now and then retain some inoffensive emblem.
So stubborn, nothing will remain of him.
Even the body under the steadfast measure of a mean-spirited tempo grows reckless and, too taut the musical string, it breaks . . .
. . .

And everything tends towards chaos.
Ah, vivre libre ou mourir!

Irony

I listen to the season of spring opening among the black aching branches.
This is the only hour at which I can follow it, walking past the houses alone with their thoughts.
It is the hour of shuttered windows, yet
this sadness of returnings has taken me from sleep.
Tomorrow morning a verdant veil will touch upon these trees, still dry when night fell a moment ago.
God does not grant peace.
Only at this hour is given, to a few rare dreamers, the torment of following such work.
Tonight, although it is April, snow is falling upon the city.
No violence is surpassable that has the appearances of silence and cold.

A Recurring Dream

> The Nile overcast
> the dark beauties
> robed in water
> laughing at the carriages
>
> Escaping

Lucca

In my house, in Egypt, after supper, the rosary recited, my mother spoke to us of these parts.
I spent my childhood spellbound.
The city traffic is punctilious and fanatical.
Within these walls it's only possible to be en route.
Here the objective is to leave.
I'm sitting outside the door of a caffè with some people who talk to me of California as if it were a parcel of their own.
In terror I discover myself in the traits of these types.
Now I feel pulsating through my veins, the hot blood of my dead.
I too have held a hoe.
Between the smoking thighs of the earth I catch myself laughing.
Farewell desires and nostalgias.
I know of the past and the future all that a man can know.
Now I recognize my destiny, and my origin.
There's nothing left for me to profane, nothing for me to dream.
I've enjoyed it all, and suffered.
There's nothing left for me except to resign myself to dying.
I shall raise therefore my children in tranquillity.
When a malignant appetite urged me on to mortal loves, I celebrated life.
Now that I consider, *even I,* love to be a safeguard of the species, death is in my sights.

Revelation of the Woman

Now the woman appeared to me unveiled, in a natural modesty.
Since then her movements, liberated, ascending in a fecund solemnity, consecrate me to the only real sweetness.
In such confident intimacy I can continue without weariness.
At any moment night may fall, and lunar limpidity newly make bare the shadows.

Prayer

When I awake
from the blinding light of promiscuity
to a limpid, astonished sphere

When my weight has to me grown lighter

Grant me O Lord that shipwreck
at the first cry of that opening day.

—

It has been suggested that "L'Affricano a Parigi" may be a reworking of the subject matter of the poet's 1916 "In memoria" whose setting, though written in Locvizza, is indeed Paris. In a non-contemporary note Ungaretti says the locale of the later poem is, in fact, Milan, or a synthesis of various European cities

ÉDOUARD GLISSSANT

translated from the French

SEASONS

in Snow 10, Spring 2022

Complete section of *Le sang rivé*, 1947–1954
in *Poèmes Complets*, Gallimard, Paris, 1994
entitled «Saisons»

Glory

to Jacques Charpier

The queens of the new blue azur arise unbridled from their lands.
River of foliages, and route of the morning,
From the dawn itself, from the blue azure, and the beasts whinneying,
I saw you were made glorious and saddened old words,
And this mirage this conflagration,
Mares now so familiar, and tamed.

You have gathered, in the manner of a druid in the supernatural forest of the past,
A noon. And the hour and the future they married, their wedding all to your liking, sweet.

Flames. Charges at the gates of noon. May this whole song
Of muds and clays and rivers descending the plumbline of the day
Place you in a place of order, of thirst, neither feasting nor lightning blindness
May this lure lead you not into the harvesting of a *viscaceae* of yesteryear.

To Die, Not To Die

to Jean Laude

Perfumes have dried on the sands of my stars. Foam from the heights no longer dazzles, there the tome, and its harvest.

Parchments of paths where water is rare, the book of the Dead and Lethes, in the lands of the North invaded with vendanges, underground O underground.

Open, nights are splendid in the Book. (Sea measured in fruits and salt. The summer of night lights the summer.)

I'm learning I'm learning that here is a battle, later love never returns, it's dead; the field is deserted, here there wasn't a combatant, only long-drawn-out defeat.

So watch the water as it washes the dead; his wife sloshed it under the foot of the clergy.
Death and his ferrymen are forsworn
For leaving the heart the immense sea it begins.

Temptations

to Paul Mayer

   Lassoes you leave us in the white day whiter than the summer snow
   The blind whereon your bodies pass past dreams, here you lash the salt
to so many washed-up storms

   If it's love the words flare up tear apart you wander lost
   For you love infringes the sky and you have only depths
   And you have only caves and cliffs for your desperate bodies

   If it's tillage you prevail you are snow under the bast
   What do you say when you sleep beneath thickness within fibre
   You who so disturb and delight us?
   Or are you nothing but phantoms inhabited by impure wakes
   Or are you only lassoes yourselves, to assail and tempt us?

Solitude

to Roger Giroux

Mast the snow has lashed fast with silence
At the beach and the sudden evaporation of the salt
It recognizes the sea breaks the shore front
Escapes the wind where moons warm to one.

Night comes it comes sat like a white toril
On the breast stirred by a wind of prophesies
It unburies neither a vase of furies nor a blue love
Only an absence of light.

O perfection of defeat O law of the dawn
The wind the solitary has wed the wave returned it
In the chalice of its soma a sweetness
So like a son to caress.

Daughters of the sea! Men of salt! Gods propitious at the fêtes!
O never-ending nuptials.

Beauty

to Max Clarac-Sérou

It's here there's a wind of solemn roses it's blue azure
Woven into a flowering of irrealities, such lovely hands
It's the summer stripped of its dream by the wind, naked child
Sobbing at daybreak awaiting noon.

Your city discerns you. Hardly a word implores this invisible
Breeze obliging us to boast of transparencies
And more secret in its sap and unspeakable. Look,
Salt restores the season, the roseate trees, the child.

Roses of irreality we speak the impure incense.

GUNNAR EKELÖF

translated from the Swedish

POEMS & PROSE

in Snow 3, Spring 2015

"Röster under jorden" from "Två fristående dikter"
in *Om hösten* (Stockholm, Bonniers, 1951)

"Non serviam" and
"From things to sounds" title in English in the original
from "Dikter vid skilda tillfällen 1930–45"
in *Non servium* (Stockholm, Bonniers, 1945)

"Eufori" from "Fuga"
in *Färjesång* (Stockholm, Bonniers, 1941)

reprinted in a.o.
Skrifter 1: Dikter 1927–1954 (Stockholm, Bonniers, 1991)

Although archaeopteryx features in "Röster under jorden" the image shown on page 40 does not accompany the poem but appears as the last page of Ekelöf's *En Mölna-elegi: Metamorfoser* (Stockholm, Bonniers, 1960) reprinted in a.o. *Skrifter 2: Dikter 1955–1962* (Stockholm, Bonniers, 1991)

Voices Under the Earth

The hours pass. Time passes.
It is late or early for different people.
It is late or early for different light.
—Silently the morning light jars the drug of sleep
and shelves it away in all the pharmacies
(with their black-white-checkered floors)—
colourless and dawn-bitter
myself tired as never years and days until death . . .
—I long from the black square to the white.
—I long from the red thread to the blue.

That young man! (there is something wrong with his face)—
That pale girl! (her hand is in the flowers at the window:
she exists only together with her hand
which only exists together with . . .)
The bird that flies and flies. With its flight.
Someone who hides. Others who only exist together with the other.
The old woman sneaking around and around until she is discovered.
Then slyly smiling she turns and retires.
But she comes back.
The caretaker at the desk (stained in well-worn pinegrain). He has no eyes.
The child turned toward the blackboard, always turned to the blackboard.

The pointer's screech. Where is the hand?
It is in the flowers at the window.
The smell of chalk. What does the smell of chalk say to us?
That the hours pass, time passes.
That slowly the morning light pulverizes the drug of sleep . . .
. . . with their black-white-checkered floors—

Archaeopteryx! What a lovely name!
Archaeopteryx! My bird!
—Why does it chirrup so unhappily?
—It chirrups about its life, wants to fly away, has perhaps already flown.
I have already fondled it as a stone.
With thousand-year beats my stone heart beat in my veins.
Perhaps there were petrified birds and lizards in there!
Rhamphornycus! Archaeopteryx!
In a new light the stone became a living bird and flew off
but now and then out of duty or habit it comes back.
Someone is always left behind, that is the horror.
—Iguanodon!
The bird is gone but says it is still here—is that to protect itself?
How can it still be here? It is not here. It is you who are still here.
The bird is free. It is you who wait.
I wait.
I long for the bird that flies and flies
with its flight.
Myself I am bound to the stone. The age-old stone.

Lately the bird has complained that it cannot sleep.
Who can sleep?
I woke the bird one night—it was indoors.
I woke it because my thoughts were plaguing me.

I wanted to know.
The bird says it flies away in order to give me a much greater happiness—
A diplomatic fight for freedom!
I fondled a stone. I became a stone.
I was the last piece in the jigsaw
the piece that didn't fit anywhere, the picture complete without me.
Something is always left over, that is the horror.

Everything turned inside out in me, everything vaporized.
The bird took my wings and gave them to another light.
It went out. It was dark.
Archaeopteryx! Archaeopteryx!
I groped around me, got nothing in my hands
nothing to remember, nothing to forget . . .
—Is there no forgetfulness in the house of the abyss?
—Not when everything is abyss.
—Is there no light?
—Not when it is out.
—Is it day or night?
—It is night.
—How hard the lamps stare!
—They watch over the stones.
—So far below the surface!
—There is no surface.
But there, on the bed, I see a solitary limestone among the fish . . .
Deaf, dumb they circle around in their own light.
It has no light.
It has no bed.
It cannot close its eyes over someone's joy.
It cannot open them.
—This is hell!
—No, it is emptiness.

And the house of the stars is empty
and the souls
draw away from the universe—
Slowly and indifferently the earth wraps time around its axis,
more tensile than some elastic band.
Your feet have to take the endlessly winding spiral staircase,
the stair spindle that twists dizzily like a wide-eyed dream

from landing to landing, from stair-tread to stair-tread of stone . . .
You hold your head still:
You are forced to take the stair-treads one at a time and your body twists:
You twist your head.
You suffocate in stone, suspended in viscous stone, in which you sleep.
Birds and molluscs sleep there like you
with lizards and flowers,
and even raindrops sleep
on pillows of stone, under sheets of stone.
With thousand year beats their hearts of stone beat
in veins of stones.
For a billion billion years time swirls them with itself
in raging storms of stones through seas of stone
to skies of stone . . .
—What am I? Where are you?
—Wake up!
—In the house of the abyss.
—Is there no obliviousness in the house of the abyss?
—Not one's own but others'.
And all these homeless patients who drift around the day rooms
have only walls for doctors.
A zigzag of temperature charts covers the barred off doors.
Everything lies on its back, everything turns
again and again on its back. No one knows
what is up or down. Everything turns
again and again on its back,
even the chairs, even walls and floors.
Everything turns.
Everyone's eyes are blank and as empty as windows,
one sees neither night nor day . . .
—Is it night or day?
—It is night

and the night rests mirroring and black against the windowpanes.
The night rises, the night is soon on the fourth floor.
The night is soon on the fifth floor.
The night is soon on the sixth floor.
Now the night is on the seventh floor.
—How many floors are there?
—A lot.
—What tremendous pressures against the windowpanes on the ground floor!
Should they shatter the night would rush in,
fill the rooms with darkness, rise from floor to floor!
—Keep to the side up there on the stairs!
—What's with the push and shove!
—No tarrying!
There is a throbbing in the radiators as if a heart were straining,
the lamps go dead when they act out the opposite
and try to hold back the darkness.
A white loneliness against a black loneliness.
Or a black loneliness against a white loneliness.
And while the darkness swirls round the gables of the house
from all these lonelinesses comes cry after cry of silence:
—Who are you, shadow at the pine-stained desk?
—Death was left sitting at his place like a wretched caretaker.

> The hours pass. Time passes.
> Slowly the morning light pulverizes the drug of sleep.
> —I long from the black square to the white.
> —I long from the red thread to the blue.

From Things to Sounds

Very odd transactions are underway just now in my vicinity. In my ears I still hear the Prime Minister's raised, adamantine cadence: "No, not even a thirty!" from the car in which he sits with the door open onto the curb, in a dress suit, as my new-found friend, who calls him his "quarter-uncle" and who is son to some other kind of bigwig, leans down over the car door in an attempt to borrow money off him, while asking me to move a few steps to one side. I think: he's not shy that one. One sort of society is no better than the other.

I would not have allowed myself to remain in such a faux situation if I had not just gone arm in arm with his sister. She is delightful, trusting, utterly unspoilt, and her evening gown, her soft, shiny, well-groomed hair bun about her neck (1939 model), do nothing but add perverse touches to the aura she has around her of a log driver's bride from Ådalen. Now that she's standing obliquely in front of me on the gardens' path I can most discreetly cast a caressing glance at her back. Compared with her brother there is really nothing to be said.

A little later in the evening I am sitting alone, very much alone, in a kind of round ivory tower, like a villa tower on top of a wooden house, in the midst of composing music. I have an instrument somewhere but I hear the music around me, how it rises, towering up, building ever higher and higher. It is a two-tone orchestral piece, part of a symphony, the relationship between the keys is more-or-less C sharp minor for the left hand and B flat major for the right. It sounds as if I had Bach in my right hand, a slow solemn Bach, and a Swedish folk air in my left hand, a funny sort of Swedish folk air. As I said, it is a sketch for a symphony and there and then I think up the legend: "Puisque vous ne voulez que de grandes machines, en voici un éléphant!"

Now that gives me more of a whiff of the Hector Berlioz'. But when I woke up, even with the music in my head, it was another thing altogether, I do remember.

Euphoria

You sit in the garden alone with a notebook, a sandwich, flask and pipe.
It is night but so calm that the light burns without flickering,
spreads its reflection over the table of rough-hewn planks
and glistens in the bottle and the glass.

You take a draught, a bite, you fill and light your pipe.
You write a line or two and pause a moment to contemplate
the streak of sunset red sailing toward the morning red,
the sea of wild chervil, a green-white foam in the summer night's dusk,
not a single moth around the light but choruses of gnats in the oak,
leaves so still against the sky . . . And the aspen that rustles in the stillness:
All nature strong with the love and death around you.

As if this were the last evening before a long, long voyage:
The ticket is in one's pocket and the packing is done.
And you can sit and sense the distant land's closeness,
sense how everything is in everything, at the same time its end and its beginning,
sense that here and now are both leavetaking and homecoming,
sense how death and life are strong like the wine within you!

Yes, to be one with the night, one with myself, with the light's flame
as it looks me quietly in the eyes, unfathomable and quiet,
one with the aspen rustling and whispering,
one with the flocks of flowers leaning out of the darkness and listening
to something I had on the tip of my tongue to say that never got said,
something I don't want to let out even if I could.
And that murmurs within me of the purest joy!

And the flame rises . . . As if the flowers pressed closer,
closer and closer in shimmering flecks of rainbow.
The aspen quivers and dances, the evening red sails
and everything that was unsayable and distant is unsayable and close.

    I sing of the only thing that syncretizes,
    the only practical, for all alike.

Non Serviam

I am a stranger in this land
but this land is no stranger in me!
I am not at home in this land
but this land behaves as if it were at home in me!

    *

I have in me a blood that can never be diluted
a tumbler full in my veins!
And always the Jew, the Lapp, the artist in me
seeks his blood brother: searches in the writings
makes a detour round the seite in the wilderness
in wordless reverence for something forgotten
joik in the wind: Savage! Nigger!—
butt and shout at the stones; Jew! Black!—
outside the law and within the law:
imprisoned in theirs, the Whites, and still
  —praise be my law!—in mine!
                                    /

Thus I have become a stranger in this land
but this land has made itself at ease in me!
I cannot live in this land
but this land lives like bane in me!

Once, in the brief, the mild
the poor whiles' wild Sweden
there was my land! It was everywhere!
Here, in the long, the well-fed whiles'
tight and cosy Sweden
where everything is sealed against draughts . . . to me it's cold.

—

Glossary to "Non Serviam"
seite Sami ancient cult stone
joik Sami traditional song style

—

CLAUDE ROYET-JOURNOUD

translated from the French

from
USAGE AND ATTRIBUTES OF THE HEART
INTIMATE TRANSITION FROM THE EVENT

A MATERIAL ROCKING, DISPOSITION

in Snow 10, Spring 2022

Opening section of ten in
L'usage et les attributs du cœur
Transition *intime* de l'événement
P.O.L.
2021

Trees are nothing more than points constructing a shadow. Let's add a sentence to sleeping. Beset by freckles. Diaphanous earth. How can they dominate the landscape without wavering? I want to show you, she says. You see the tree, over there? That's ours. Come, we'll follow the edge. You see the pond? There too, by the tall trees. It's vast. So then, home! We haven't seen each other for how many years? Different face, same voice same accent. When I left, she stayed on, alone, by the side of the path.

behind a tarpaulin
the work of shadows

almost not laid over this little body

a puppet can no longer dance

mother's foot is bare

with the red top of this triangle
he would love to open the scene

backward with his hand

a sentence to bury the body

No image can remedy this. *Circumscribed by other accidents*, furrowed with dust, the lake assumes a dark delay which alters breathing. Missing words are a dirty thing, stuck to the wall. In this land of lacets and lagoons, stones are sown. We divide the impossible.

    to perform these acts
    postures have to be described

    dispose of human odour
    bring boards of uneven length

    a gathering at the foot of the steps
    in preparation for the exercise

    the women arrive from outside
    the suppression of tears renders the air more breathable

    suicide smacks a few of them with amazement

    why is not a word

    you are asleep in the light

you keep the day as a threat
at the juncture of the plains
forget the appearance of this envelope
its absence of cause
get used to being the only one in the photograph

a break-in
born of tenderness

ANDREA ZANZOTTO

translated from the Italian

Ten below zero and rosepink

in *Snow 5, Fall 2017*

Dieci sotto zero e rose in
Sovrimpressioni, Mondadori, 2001

I

O such sweet snows rosepink-petal colour
petal of glacial daybreak
rosepink colour of easter egg
and which in motionless circuit served as stairs
to a more distant, but imminent comet . . .   HALE-BOPP
You made our dearest and lovely laid down mountain mammae
hyperbolically free, even if from themselves
as from all nature-conjecture
within reach even as an immature vista
From where a similar voracious Perfection
and Seedsleep of rosepink and Indifference
and the Calm of rosepink?   Banquet of dragées.
Promise of rosepink.   Cruelty of rose-spouse-pink.
Numerous nutritious mounts
and ever mocking making concrete
distracted so much from their habitual zodiac
hastened frazzle of single and multiple rosepink
left half-open   like a thousand phrases
but without conviction but tender-terrible stasis
Absolute election of ever seen absolute of rosepink
Divulged essence of effusions and delusions
of Rosepink-Torment in Early-rosepink
    in Below-rosepink
      finally destabilized sacred tic
      definitive act with ding-ding of Caina
      rosepink of refined intimacy   USTRINA

II

Repeated and volatile appeals of the rosepink
across the sheets of the daylight calendar
confined in surprise whose unspoiled lips
                          unspoiled rachis-lips
denied a few moments later
happy with a backslide
to the random to the divinely bygone
happy with their non said
possibles and impossibles
and all conceivable ferments
in the vitriolic excess, in the surplus
Were-are-shall-shall-no-longer-be:
all in the same light timeliness
               timeliness and cluster of rosepink tempo
               forgotten rosepink
               of TIME and "tempo" of rosepink
               summations of time
               sources as individual
               as whole rosepink
I sink in that rosepink
curse that rosepink
return to my beyond of that rosepink
     (invite you dismiss you in that rosepink)
          (annul you in that rosepink)
               (industrious, there we are refreshed in that rosepink)

—

VICTOR SEGALEN

translated from the French

FIVE PAINTINGS

in Snow 4, Spring 2016

In his dedication in *Peintures* (1916) to Georges Daniel de Monfreid Segalen writes: *Ces Peintures, littéraires*. The "Five Paintings" here were not included in *Peintures* and remained unpublished until issued in a limited edition by Thierry Bouchard in 1981. They were added as an appendix to *Peintures* (Gallimard, 1983, 1996) but are not included in *Paintings* (Quartet, 1991) and are translated here for the first time

Mirror

> *Surprise & mysterious in a mirror without a subject. On the beyond of a mirror. Magic mirrors, so sensitive that every Carving on the Back shimmers through to the polished front. —*

    A quick glance at this bronze grey mirror, —from the time of the Han, —of course I know we cannot call what we see in a mirror exactly "painting". But we have said "magic" the reflections that this particular one and a few others reflect. —Look at yourself in this small round mirror, which is barely able to contain your face, diminished. —It's a perfectly polished surface, isn't it; of leaded silver hue, slightly bumped, and soft to the touch: a disc of grey light. Look at yourself: in the midst of your remote and reflected image, there they are, jumbled, hazy yet distinct, the animals of the zodiac, divination squares, roses, celestial bodies. Nonetheless the surface is perfectly clear and polished to a т. Do these signs emanate from you? No, but on the other side of the mirror: turn it round: it gifts you all the mysteries of its decoration through a heavy rim of forged metal: faintly, but distinctly, it unveils the fullness of its intimate splendour, which it blends with the reflection it receives. Wasn't I right to say: a magic mirror?

Painted in Blood

These sketches, done with a single dark red stroke, can hardly be called Paintings. —There's no more spun silk, even and soft, nor chalky colours or blue porphyry or antique turquoise, crushed. The painter's tool here is not the pliant brush, as thick as a stylus, as supple as living hair; —but only the living finger, the finger cut by sorcery and exuding its colour; or the finger dipped in blood. These are just sketches in blood. Nothing is drawn here in the tranquility of the study, but at the red moments of life. We do not know the nature of the fever that spurted in chrysanthemums. —The wove is at once delicate and severe: a creamy paper, soft, pulpy, porous to the touch, which handsomely arrays the contours.

It is a cushiony bed where the touch is impressed; where the pressure shows the strike of the finger. —But, here! What erupted is dark red, immediate, bloody and brusque! —Like sometimes, in the past, the masters loved to play with the ink, and tip the pot over in order to trace out (or with a single finger, and an unbroken gesture): a mountain, a beggar, an inspirited genius, a conqueror, a limping hero . . . Here, the unnamed painter has trailed his finger across the barely dry paste. But that finger was swollen with blood. Probably his own. There are examples of this. Some besieged peoples had only their finger for a brush and their blood as colour. And all such fireworks are precious. They are painful or atrocious gestures. They are moments congealed under a dark brown mass. We cannot see any softness there: this is painted in jets of blood.

Some Silence

Others have sought through violent confrontations, fireworks, commotions of brushes, chrysanthemums of ink to simulate the loudest noise. This displays only silence. —A woman, her eyes fixed, lacklustre, her eyes blank; a trembling and delicate face but motionless; —a lip without words . . . and even, not even her breath releases her fl-flourish and sibilant vapour into the air. —Far off, soldiers, swords unsheathed, are searching every cranny of the palace. —Motionless, the woman doesn't move, doesn't breathe, and, from the firmness of the features of her bosom, you can see clearly that her heart isn't even beating. —She is seated, *half-clothed*, beside her grand imperial robe thrown there beside her, which also forms a heap of air and silence . . . Nothing moves; nothing cries, nothing grizzles: the soldiers are still searching, far off, so their footfalls are muffled. Not a sound. —We cannot hear anything here, can we!

Oh! It's because this woman has magic powers. Taking in her arms the newborn of Heaven they are searching for to slay, she beseeches him thus: "If you are of the true race of Chu!" and it has to go on: "do not cry!" —and covered him with her discarded robe . . .

And for as long as they are here, for as long as you are watching, —believe me, you will hear nothing. —

Chinese Stained Glass

If some Master-Painter in the China of Antiquity had wanted to do this—don't worry, he would have. If he had dared, instead of silk and gum, and water, to use luminous glass, with colour melted in liquid glass, —he would have done so . . . Why not do what he did not dare to do? A Chinese stained-glass window! The whole antique decoration transparent! Look! Look closely, this is only a hypothesis, but the most beautiful, the most obvious, the most picturesque of all! If China had wanted stained glass in its large picture windows as the face of the house . . . Palaces were built for that! The façade is, in construction, transparent! Between the floor and the roofs, the entire façade transmits the sun; the roof frowns under the summer sun; it completely raises the lid on the shy wintery eye . . . If China had just dared, it might have had stained glass. It had known coloured glass, bluish, iridescent; it had known the fixing of colour by fire; and the stained-glass window is the igniting of colour by fire and in the sun! That's how we could have seen it . . .

This one, among many others: A south-facing façade . . . under the great roof, in the imperial sun: from inside we could have seen this: the sun, striking the flagstones, —but transparent; —a crush of colours on hard transparent surfaces . . . There are contributions from afar, strange, —yet transparent. It is the entire *tribute to Yu*, it is an *audience*, —yet transparent. The beasts of burden have stopped at the periphery and [are you looking for the Emperor?] he's the one who's watching! and the porters; —more to the centre, the [. . .]. Next we are looking, Facing South, for the Emperor—Impossible to see him, because he's the one who's watching it all. All That, in the Noonday sun.

. . . But . . . After that what painting will last? What ceiling? What pride? What man?

Yes, probably, the Masters of China were wise, not to address the sun, scintillant Emperor of the Sky. Nevertheless, we can address the sun. What painting will last? None, except for the ones that follow.

The show isn't over...

The show isn't over. But it is inside yourself and I cannot let you in! The four seasons have passed, and still you believe in the full Year? or, like the symbol sometimes suggests, in the fulfilment of life? Then you would be very close to the end of life, and old and grey watching this changing picture in the skies? No—If you are a really good spectator, if you know how to see, know that time will skate around you without affecting you. This is the sensitive and delicate point in the play I have invited you to. Know that beyond all the seasons there is one that the play of moons cannot control, that does not achieve its equilibrium at the hour of the solstice, one that no official astronomer can either name or measure. Likewise, in noting the cardinal points, to the Fifth, centre and middle which is the self, the Fifth season has no age and is missing from the calendar. It lives inside us, it faces off ourselves. Even after this freezing yet nonetheless comforting display of winter, —even after the full cycles of the others, it is down to us, really down to us to see it, no longer in the clouds but in the well deep within us. From now on it's in fun that the other four revolve around it, its different images, lost reflections in the skies.

—

CESARE PAVESE

translated from the Italian

Five Poems

from

Work Wears You Down

in Snow 11, Spring 2023

Lavorare stanca, Einaudi, 1943

The poems' original titles are
"Paternità", "Lavorare stanca", "Maternità", "Paternità" and
"Lo steddazzu", which is regional Calabrian, though the poem
itself is in Italian, hence an effort at a sort of match, here in Scots

"Paternità" and "Maternità" are also titles of sections of the book
"Lavorare stanca" is the second of two poems so titled

Lavorare stanca, Solaria, 1936, was a smaller collection, which should
have included the first three poems here, except that "Paternità" was
one of a few poems deleted by the censor on grounds of morality

Pavese wrote in an essay about his work, "each poem, a story"

Fatherhood

Fantasia of the dancing woman, of the old man
who is her father, who once held her in his veins
and sired her on a joyful night, in a bed, ah, naked.
She hurries to get there to undress, because those
other old men are waiting too. Together they
devour her, when she leaps out to dance, all eyes alight
on those powerful legs, but the old men tremble.
Almost naked the young girl. The young men look on
smiling, and quite a few wish they were naked.

They all look like her father those eager old men
they are all, unsteady, a remnant of a body
that once enjoyed other bodies. These young men too will
one day become fathers, woman for them is one woman.
It happened in silence. An intense joy
grasps the darkness in front of the living girl.
All bodies are but one, one alone
whose movement pins down everyone's gaze.

This blood, which courses through the girl's
lovely limbs, is the same blood that coagulates in the old;
and her father smoking in silence, warming himself,
doesn't dance, but he sired this daughter who does.
There's a feeling and a zip in her body
just as in the old man, and the other old men. Silently
her father smokes waiting for her to return, dressed.
Everyone is waiting, the young and the old, staring at her;
and each one, drinking alone, will think of her again.

Work Wears You Down

Crossing a street to run away from home
is something only a kid would do, but this man walking
the streets all day isn't a kid any more
and he's not running away from home.

                                                         There are summer
afternoons when even the squares are empty, languid
under a setting sun, and this man, walking
along an avenue planted with useless shrubs, pauses.
Is it worth this being alone, to be more and more alone?
Just going round, squares and streets
empty. You need to approach a woman
and talk to her and decide to live together.
Otherwise, you're talking to yourself. This is why there are
times at night when a drunk accosts you
and lays out before you his whole life's story.

It's certainly not by hanging around a deserted square
that you'll meet anyone, but walking in the streets
people do occasionally stop. If they were two,
even walking along the street, home would be
wherever the woman was and that would be worth it.
Night-time and the square is once again deserted
and the man, crossing it, doesn't see the houses
between the useless lights, he no longer lifts his eyes:
he's conscious only of the pavement, which other men have made
with their hardened hands, like his own.
There's no point moping about in a deserted square.
There'll certainly be that woman in the street
who, if he asked, would lend a hand at home.

Motherhood

This is a man who has sired three sons: a large powerful
body, sufficient unto itself; to see him pass by,
you would imagine his sons to be built like him.
They must have issued, already formed, straight
from the limbs of their father (the woman does not count)
three young men just like him. But no matter how,
not one iota of the father's limbs is missing
not a scrap: they detached themselves from him
walking by his side.

               The woman was there,
a woman healthy in body, who spilled
her blood on each of her boys, and on the third she died.
It seems strange to the three young men to live without the woman
whom no one knows and who bore them, each one, with difficulty
annihilating herself in them. The woman was young
she laughed and she talked, but it's a risky game
taking part in life. And that's how it was that the woman
kept silent, dumbstruck staring at her man.

The three sons have a way of shrugging their shoulders
that the man recognizes. None of them
knows that they have in their eyes and in their bodies a life
that once was rich and satisfied that man.
But, seeing one of his youngsters at the river's edge about
to dive in, that man no longer sees the flash
of her limbs in the water, and the joy
of two submerged bodies. He no longer sees his sons
when he sees them in the street and compares them with himself.
How long has it been since he sired his sons? The three young men
swagger about and one of them by accident
has gone and fathered a son, without holding to the woman.

Fatherhood

A solitary man facing a useless sea,
waiting for evening, waiting for morning.
Children are playing there, but this man would like to
have a child of his own and watch him play.
Monster clouds make a palace on the water
ruined and resurrected day after day, colouring
the children's faces. The sea will always be there.

Morning wounds. Across the humid beach
the sun crawls, clinging to nets and stones.
The man sets out in the murky sun and walks
along the sea. He does not look at the scummy foams
breaking on the shore never finding peace.
At this hour the children are still drowsing
in the warmth of the bed. At this hour a woman
drowsing under the covers, would make love
if she were not alone. Slowly, the man strips
naked like the far away woman, and plunges into the sea.

Then the night, which melts the sea, and you listen
to the vast emptiness beneath the stars. Children
in the roseate houses are falling asleep
and some are crying. The man, weary with waiting,
lifts his eyes to the stars, which hear nothing.
There are women at this hour who undress a child
and put them to sleep. Someone in a bed is
embracing a man. From the black window
comes a raucous gasp, and no one hears it
except the man who knows all the tedium of the sea.

Starn o' the Mornin

The solitary man gets up while the sea is still dark
and the stars twinkling. A warm breath
rises from the shore, where the sea bed is,
to ease his breathing. This is the hour when nothing
can happen. Even the pipe clenched between his teeth
is spent. A gentle nocturnal lapping.
The solitary man has already lit a bonfire of branches
and watches it mantle the ground. Before long
even the sea will be like the fire, ablaze.

Nothing is more bitter than the dawning of a day
in which nothing will happen. Nothing is more bitter
than futility. Wearily suspended in the sky
is a green tinged star, surprised by the dawn.
It sees the still dark sea and the patch of the fire
where the man, for something to do, is warming himself;
it sees, and sinks in sleep among the sombre mountains
with their bed of snow. The slowness of the hour
is merciless, for those who wait for nothing more.

Is it worth it that the sun rise from the sea
and the long day begin? Tomorrow
the warm dawn will return with its diaphanous light
and it will be like yesterday and nothing will ever happen.
The solitary man will want only to sleep.
When the last star goes out in the sky,
taking his time the man prepares his pipe and lights it.

ROGER GIROUX

translated from the French

Should memory CEASE

in Snow 8, Spring 2020

« Si la mémoire CESSE » first published in
K.O.S.H.K.O.N.O.N.G., no. 16, printemps 2019, revue
dirigée par Jean Daive, chez Éric Pesty Éditeur
Copyright © K.O.S.H.K.O.N.O.N.G. 2019
for the Estate of Roger Giroux

Written possibly between 1970–1973

SETTING NOTE

Two English phrases in the original are here enclosed [ ]
occurences of JE, JE, rather than Je, je, are here small cap I
one occurence of Je, rather than je, within a sentence, is
here [I]; ovals and a rectangle around phrases are freehand
in the original, not regular as here; the original is untitled
the first page is by way of a statement, followed by a blank

Should memory CEASE

Event

Cage

or well aware of my estrangement in
         the learned ranges of
the air, without air, precipice, outside.

Then to be drowned in the contraction
         of a single unpronounceable
final
sound?

So . . .
         yet to see?
yet from here? yet the heart?
beyond the burnt-out lamp?
Even its terror?
knotted? Denied?

Shall I begin?
In some other time, in another language,
         the one body in my tomb,
         shall see? →

*

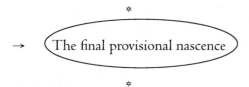

*

Fire is foolish. Affright the silence of the soul. Prevent the interior listening. Infernal, yes.

*

Awaken senses, lance desires

*

In silence, the walls are worse.

Thus.

First, make a fire. To ward off the ghosts of absence. For the voice to disimmure and fill the space inside and the space outside.

But can you make a Book of Nothing? Of the pain of this nothing?

This nothing! And here already I am giving it presence, a face, just about. *This* looks at me and summons me in silence, a gaping mouth poking out its knotted delicate tongue. I look at *this*, draw it, touch its image, as if tracing with the tip of my finger the contour of a mouth about to be taken, lips, tongue, and when the teeth get stuck in there, thirty-two cries will rip the page.

---

to say oh, of what, and what, strangely
this star, to myself

and hums, hums
in its icy naming

(stone: is it possible?)

the soul, searching for it
through dark starvations—
it, that unworked it
that we are

it might be winter
in its ravenous decay

to touch it

(stone, similar, so much: seeing!)

and the air,
the air that we are.
Then descend naming
Heart
Blade
Highness fast

behind the sabulous

far off
a great wall of ah
(why?)

and breaks
to the quick

desire
distance
the NON (said?)

(destroy what inhabits it)

then the image clouds

and, in the dark
wait for the ear
to fade.

To write it

mauve
like, sometimes
even

and, from a so long sun
make a lake
between the fingers of the Immortelle?

Don't stifle the silence.
Open your hand:
Jump!

The space that keeps quiet
inhabits your voice.
Here is right
there

As if everything came from the silence
nourishing
The invisible never
of the rose

*   Have we lost the key
    to the unforgettable
    number and mirror

    is this Céline's room
    where a very pure, very wise, eye swims,
    or a Blackcap's that wanted
    to rip off its face
    to be stark naked?

    *(ten years of light
    for a single grain of sand.)*

    descend
    between the trees
    in September dark
    where your voice seeks its colour.

    you can, that far.

Here lies, outside

a place toward the closed
distance

and this
in

---

8 pm. Four hours, shouldn't it be possible for me to write, say, twenty poems? Why this certitude no? Would they come to me from experience? Never, in 30 years (thirty years . . . !) did such a phenomenon occur. I have known states of high tension (rarely, increasingly) but what did I judge worth keeping? I'm speaking of twenty poems of a superior essence if I dare say it. But that's to play with a notion of quantity, while I am inclined only toward the excellent, efficacious, absolute, word, toward the unattainable Unique Poem → hence non-making which overwhelms me more each year, which disturbs me, having

no more desire for this foolishness of measuring myself against the Impossible known, to be sure. Desire, if, even so, yet disillusioned. But the desire is there, under masks I no longer hardly dare peel off. And even as I write this, it is a sort of cowardice, a sign of weariness, and a warding off of the anguish that sometimes, today, physically disgusts me. No other motion appeals to me. Reading, travelling, spending time with others are just as dull to me. Including this house which no longer pleases me, a simple shell welling only with boredom . . . (Still, I know, certain landscapes: some mountains, a lake and firs, a thousand places in the world that have never disappointed me; but where I escaped myself; I was no longer in myself, only in the gaze of a beauty I did not seek to capture, to dismember, only pure acceptance of what is, there, here, in a disposition in which I can share only if I give myself up to it, outside myself, in another word, in the word of the Other—whose absence laughs in my face if I summon it.)

Twenty minutes have come and gone. I have lit, smoked a cigarette. I have not come close to the Poem with a single line. I have shaken off the veil that was suffocating me. Does writing have some medicinal virtue? Only that?

This writing just skims the crest of the waves, which is only an exudation, a facile piece of vomit, a letter to a shadow of myself. Writing, yes, but to the shadow of the Other, this Other I've already spoken about, with its other needs. Writing is Need itself. Writing needs Everything, and never agrees to anything. [Writing is a non-rewarding activity.] The "satisfactions" the poet is able to draw from his activity are the dross of a world that Poetry does not address. Isn't the Poem itself a useless residue of this act? And yet, it demands of me all of its powers, all of its substance, [for free]! For nothing. This apparent *waste* of the best of a being, it's this, the foolishness of the Poet. (And when the Poet turns his back on writing, he feels a sense of betrayal, an unforgivable cowardice. He becomes nothing but a shadow of a shadow, an unfamiliar ghost to himself. And when he enters the Poem, he is a ghost to the world . . .)

All inadequate considerations. This writing softly cradles the non-said, the fore-making. Lazy, guilt-ridden, it buries itself in the sands of physical nothingness. Mortal, while the effort at the Poem is, inexplicably, birth and life. And even if the Poem goes so far as to kill, it affords a vital death. Inexplicably.

How does one recognize a "good", a "great" poem? What sets it apart from the mediocre? At its most demanding, at the height of tension, at the point of approaching rupture, beyond which everything becomes disorganized and collapses into an anterior nothingness. Go that far, and stop at the threshold of what can only be said by silence. The word of the Poem is the ascent —the Calvary—to silence. As far as life-death. As far as the rip.

How to bridge this distance between what I

say for the Poem and the poem itself? What is this distance? Is it located, locatable, elsewhere than in writing? It's exactly *elsewhere*—because the P. is located outside me. It turns its back on me, it looks past what I am able to with my senses, with all *my faculties*. Born of me (and of an expanding culture) it's the threshold of the beyond of me and of this culture. The P. is the necessary gate. What lies behind, no Poem will ever reveal, as if there were an interdiction, a secret to keep*. Poem, keeper of the secret..?

Embraced by the profound uselessness of all that is not It. Mystical attitude declare the critics? They don't know what they are talking about.

But what, Poem? besides words that fail?

_____

(*But further away, toward a "possible" new culture of which I am one of the voices, one of the faces—but I . . . ?)

Poem, poem . . . as if it could escape the I! At least my I is constantly present in every word. An I that I have unceasingly skinned, all the way to the abstract. Perhaps that's what I want to say, through this struggle with the Ideal Poem, the absolute. I is talking, I is speaking, outside I! P. drives I out of that space which limits its word. And I suffer to be born elsewhere, of which P. is the fearless eye. But this eye is still I whom I have not reached. Evidently it would be a good idea to keep quiet, rather than this rehash, this ludic motion of a tasteless [I] toward the uncreatable Poem. Best not to speak.

But words do not know how to dance. They are blind in an enclosed place, hunkered down, where only muffled sounds are able to reach them, a vague humming from very far back in time and whose meaning (if there ever was one) —for them was forgotten in transit. In this

I-place, (unique source) you might think they were meditating (some poor shot perhaps?)

    Work (or Poem): place-time where creation and destruction coexist. The visible moment of an equilibrium impossible to maintain. Intelligence occupies the entire distance, the inclusive space between creation from its first motion toward being and destruction until its return to nothingness. The Poem is the compression of the intelligence (Thought) to the singularity, its implosion. The Poem is the visible moment of its invisibility. Miracle of the impossible.

—

STIG DAGERMAN

translated from the Swedish

OUR NEED FOR CONSOLATION IS INSATIABLE . . .

May 1952

in Snow 7, Spring 2019

"Vårt behov av tröst är omättlig . . ."
in *Husmodern*, nr 13, Stockholm, 1952
collected in
Vårt behov av tröst: prose och poesi
P. A. Norstedt & Söners, Stockholm, 1955

I LACK FAITH and so I can never be a happy human being, for a happy human being will never need fear that life is a meaningless wandering towards a certain death. I have inherited neither a god nor a fixed point on earth, from where I might attract the attention of a god; Nor have I inherited the sceptic's well-concealed fury, the rationalist's desert mind or the atheist's burning innocence. I dare not therefore cast stones at those who believe in the things in which I doubt or at those who worship a doubt, as if it were not also shrouded in darkness. The stone would strike me myself, because of the one point about which I am firmly convinced: that humankind's need for consolation is insatiable.

Myself I hunt consolation as a hunter prey. Wherever I catch a glimpse of it in the woods I shoot. Usually I hit just empty air, but every now and then a quarry falls at my feet. Because I know that consolation's fidelity is just as fleeting as the wind's in a tree's crown I am quick to seize my catch.

What now do I hold in my arms?

Because I am alone: a beloved woman or an unhappy fellow wanderer. Because I am a poet: a self-bow of words, whose tension fills me with both joy and dread. Because I am a captive: a sudden glimpse of freedom. Because I am threatened by death: a warm living animal, a beating heart that mocks. Because I am threatened by the sea: a scarp of rock-solid granite.

But there are other consolations that present themselves like uninvited guests and fill my room with mean-spirited whisperings: I am your desire —love everyone! I am your talent—misuse it as you do yourself! I am your longing for pleasure—only gourmets are alive! I am your solitude— despise people! I am your death wish—slash!

The balance is a scantling. I see my life threatened by two forces: on one side by gluttony's voracious mouths, on the other side an avaricious bitterness feeding on itself. But I refuse to choose between orgy and asceticism, even if the price be a skin crawling with ants. It is not enough for me to know that everything is absolved under the law of involuntary will. It is not absolution for my life that I seek without what is the opposite of absolution: redemption. Finally I come to the realization that any consolation that does not admit of my freedom is illusory, is just a mirror image of my despair. For when my despair says: Inconsolable, for the day is surrounded by two nights, false consolation cries: Hope, for the night is surrounded by two days.

But human beings do not need a blague of a consolation but a consolation that enlightens. And whoever wants to be a bad human being, so to say, a human being who acts as if all actions are defensible, might at least have the courtesy to pay attention when they are that.

No one can count up all the cases when consolation is of necessity. No one knows when the shadow falls and life is not a problem to be solved by dividing light by darkness and days by nights, without an unpredictable journey between places hardly to be found. I can, for example, go down to the beach and suddenly experience eternity's terrible challenge to my existence in the sea's constant motion and the wind's constant flight. What, then, is time other than a consolation for the fact that no one human can live on—and what a wretched consolation, which only enriches the Swiss.

I might sit in front of a fire in the safest of rooms and suddenly feel how death surrounds me. It's there in the flames, in the sharp objects around me, the ceiling's weight and the walls' mass, it's there in the water, the snow, the heat and in my blood. What, then, is a feeling of human security other than a consolation for death's closeness to life—and what small consolation that only reminds us of what it would have us forget!

I might fill all my white paper with the most beautiful combinations of words that flicker in my brains. Because I long for confirmation that my life is not meaningless and that I am not alone on this earth I collect my words in a book and submit it to the world. The world in return gives me money and fame and silence. But what do I care for money and what do I care if I contribute to the advancement of literature—I care only about what I never receive: confirmation that my words have touched the world's heart. What then is my talent other than a consolation that I am alone—but what a terrible consolation which only makes me experience a fivefold loneliness!

I might see the embodiment of freedom in an animal quickly crossing a clearing and hear a voice that whispers: Live simply and take what you will and have no fear of the law! But what is this good advice other than a consolation for a freedom that does not exist—and what a pitiless consolation for those who appreciate that it takes millions of years for a human being to become a lizard!

I might finally discover that this earth is a mass grave where King Soloman, Ophelia and Himmler rest side by side. I might learn from this that the cruel and the unhappy enjoy the same death as the wise and that death might in such a way be taken as a consolation for a mistaken life. But what an atrocious consolation for those who would look to life for a consolation for death.

I have no philosophy in which I can move like a fowl in the air or a fish in the water. All I have is a duel and this duel is fought every moment of my life between false consolations, which only compound my powerlessness and deepen my despair, and true consolations, which lead me towards a monetary freedom. I should perhaps say: true consolation, because strictly speaking there is for me only one real consolation: the one that lets me know that I am a free being, an inviolable individual, one within my borders a sovereign person.

But freedom begins with slavery and sovereignty with dependency. The surest mark of my servitude is my fear of living. The definitive mark of my freedom is that my fear subsides and makes way for the even-tempered joy of independence. It may sound as if I need dependency in order finally to experience the consolation that I am a free human being, and that's certainly true. In the light of my actions I perceive that the whole of my life seems to have had the goal of acquiring millstones for my neck. The things that should have given me freedom gave me slavery and millstones instead of bread.

Other people have other masters. I, for example, am a slave to my talent to the point that I dare not use it for fear of having lost it. And when depression finally sets in I am a slave to that as well. My highest ambition is to hold on to it, my greatest desire to feel that my only value lies in what I think I have lost: the capacity to dredge beauty out of my despair, my uneasiness and my weaknesses. With bitter delight I want to see my houses fall in ruins and myself snowed in in oblivion.—But depression has seven nests and in the seventh lies a knife, a razor, a poison, a deep water and a leap from a great height. I end up becoming a slave to all these instruments of death. They follow me like dogs or I like a dog them. And I think I believe that suicide is the only attestation of human freedom.

But from a direction I could hardly have expected the miracle of being freed draws near. It might happen on the beach and the same eternity that just aroused my fear now witnesses my birth in freedom. What then does this miracle consist of? Simply the sudden realization that no one, neither powers nor people, has the right to place such demands on me that my desire to live withers. For if that desire cannot be found—what else is there?

Because I am at the sea I can learn from the sea. No one has the right to demand of the sea that it carry all the boats or of the wind that it ceaselessly fill all the sails. Likewise no one has the right to demand of me that my life shall be captive to every task. No duty above all without life! I, like everyone else, must have the right to those moments when I can step aside and feel that I am not only a part of that mass called people of the earth, but also an autonomously acting entity.

Only in that moment can I be free of all the facets of life that had previously been the cause of my despair. I know that the sea and the wind will certainly outlive me and that eternity is unconcerned about me. But who asks me to worry about eternity? My life is short only if I place it on the calendar's block. My life opportunities are limited only if I count the number of words or the number of books I shall have the time to produce before I die. But who is asking me to count? Time is a false measure of life. Time is a fundamentally worthless measuring instrument, because it extends no further than my life's façade.

But everything essential that happens to me and gives my life its wonderful content: an encounter with a beloved, the caress on the skin, help when needed, the spectacle of moonlight, sailing out to sea, the joy a child gives, a trembling before beauty, plays out lock stock and barrel outside time. For whether I meet beauty for a second or a hundred years makes no difference. Bliss sits not only side by side with time, it breaks off life's relationship with it.

So I lift the burden of time from my shoulders and thus also an obligation to perform. My life is not a thing to be measured. Neither the buck's leap nor the sunrise is a performance. A human life is no performance either but progress towards perfection. And the perfect performs nothing, it has its air of repose. It is meaningless to claim that the sea is there to carry armadas and dolphins. It certainly does that—while preserving its freedom. It is equally meaningless to claim that human beings have no other purpose than to live. Certainly one operates machines or writes books but one could just as well be doing other things. What is essential is that one does what one does while preserving one's freedom fully aware that each one of us, like every other detail in creation, is an end in oneself. At rest in oneself like a stone in the sand.

Even from the power of death I can remain free. I can certainly never be rid of the thought that death follows my steps and even less deny its actuality. But I can minimize its threat to nothing by neglecting to anchor my life to such rocky footholds as epoch and repute.

Nonetheless, it is not in my power to remain forever facing out to sea comparing its freedom with mine. The time comes when I must turn landwards and meet the orchestrators of my oppression. What I am then compelled to acknowledge is that humankind gives forms to its life, which are at least to all appearances stronger than itself. Despite all my new-found freedom I cannot crush them, only sigh beneath them. Nonetheless I recognize the demands placed on humankind that are unreasonable and those that are inevitable. One kind of freedom, I recognize, is for ever or for long over. It is the freedom that accompanies the privilege of possessing one's own element. The fish has its own, the fowl has its own, the land animal its own. Moreover Thoreau had the woods at Walden—but where are the woods in which humankind can demonstrate that it is possible to live a life in freedom outside society's rigid structures?

I am obliged to answer: Nowhere. If I want to live in freedom, it must for now be done within the structures. The world is thus stronger than I am. Against this power I have nothing to pit other than myself—but that, on the other hand, is everything. As long as I do not allow myself to be overpowered I am also a power. And my power is terrible as long as I have the power of my words to set against the world, for those who build prisons have worse plans than those who build freedom. But my power will be limitless come the day when I have only my silence to defend my inviolability, for no axe can cut the living silence.

Such is my sole consolation. I know that relapses into disconsolation are many and deep, but the memory of the miracle of being freed carries me like a wing towards the dizzying goal: a consolation that is bigger than a consolation and greater than a philosophy, namely a reason to live.

—

e Idilli
MDCCCXIX
L' Infinito
Idillio I

Sempre caro mi fu quest' ermo colle,
E questa siepe, che da tanta parte
De l'ultimo orizzonte il guardo esclude.
Ma sedendo e mirando, interminato
Spazio di là da quella, e sovrumani
Silenzi, e profondissima quiete
Io nel pensier mi fingo, ove per poco
Il cor non si spaura. E come il vento
Odo stormir tra queste piante, io quello
Infinito silenzio a questa voce
Vo comparando: e mi sovvien l'eterno,
E le morte stagioni, e la presente
E viva, e 'l suon di lei. Così tra questa
Infinità
~~Immensità~~ s'annega il pensier mio:
E 'l naufragar m' è dolce in questo mare.

Leopardi, L'Infinito, 1819, note capitalized L'I in this and other manuscripts. In line 14 Leopardi first wrote Immensità which he cancelled for Infinità before evidently restoring Immensità in print
Casa Leopardi, Recanati

GIACOMO LEOPARDI

AND

THE INFINITE

earlier version in
Antonyms Anew: Barbs & Loves, 2016
revised 2023

Over more than two hundred years since Leopardi wrote his idyll, "L'Infinito" has been translated countless times into many languages, of which at least a dozen or so are in English, not counting a number of exegeses. Why try again? Forgetting the odd clanger and howler, they all have faults of vocabulary or structure, some weirdly contorted, some serious, others less so, which is not to say that mine is perfect because it is not. For example, in lines 2–3, unhappy with the English "which" it should be, I first chose, for what I thought was resonance and fluency, "This hedgerow too, although it closes off / From view a great deal of the far horizon." but a correspondent has alerted me to its negativity where Leopardi is positive. The hedge was dear to him not despite but because it closes off the view. After many trials I have, for the moment, if apprehensively, given the hedge "density", while restoring, if ambiguously, the phrasal order of the Italian:

> I had always loved this hill on its own,[1]
> This hedgerow too, whose density a great deal
> Of the far horizon closes off from view.
> But sitting here reflecting, unending
> Spaces beyond all that, suprahuman
> Silences, and deep concerted stillness
> I picture in my mind's eye; until almost
> My heart has taken fright. And as the breeze
> I listen to rustles in these leaves, to such
> Infinite silence I begin to compare
> This song: and I summon the eternal,
> And the dead seasons, and the present
> And living, and the sound of its voice. So
> In this immensity my mind goes under:
> And my foundering at sea is sweet.

I want to home in on two words: *ermo* in the first line and *dolce* in line 15, which is the last line. They are tips of the iceberg, so to speak.

It is, I am sure, quite wrong to translate *ermo* as *lonely*, which is what the majority of translators and commentators do. The hill, the object, the subject, in Leopardi's sight, identified as Monte Tabor, little more than a stone's throw beyond Recanati, even if, even though, Leopardi has pushed it off into his imagination, is not so much *lonely* as *solitary*, which a few translators do turn to. Rare *ermo*, from the Greek, has no happy equivalence in English.[2] Naturally, one thinks of *remote*, but the hill is not really that either, nor is our English word so rare. Recognizing the difficulties, three translators go for *hermit's*, *secluded*, *lonesome*. My *on its own* is commonplace yet, rather like Lowell's elaborate *pushed off by itself*, which reveals a sentient truth, might be thought unexpected and, in that sense, rare. It seeks its own difference. Stretching it a bit I dare say. In French, Bonnefoy gives *colline solitaire* and Estève *coteau solitaire*, while Jaccottet gives *hauteur déserte*. As we see, they cannot agree the translation of *colle*. All the English translations I have read have *hill*. Might one opt for *col* as a translation of *colle* into English, thereby transferring scarcity if not rarity to the hill itself? If only, but, like *ermo* and *remote*, they are false friends, indeed opposites, *a low point*, not *a height*. Yet in *Zibaldone: The Notebooks of Leopardi* (FSG; & Penguin, 2013) we read: "Regarding the sensations that please on account of indefiniteness alone, see my idyll on the infinite, and recall the idea of a steeply sloping countryside where the view at a certain distance does not reach as far as the valley, and that of a row of trees, whose end is lost from sight, either because of the length of the row, or because it is situated in the dip, etc. etc. etc."—from Z 1430–1431 (1 August 1821). I don't think this is satisfactorily solved and I am sure there is more work to be done.

At first, I sought to avoid translating *dolce* as *sweet*. However correct, I thought there had to be a better word in English than this seemingly weak one, for all sorts of sugary reasons. But no, *sweet* is absolutely essential. It must be appreciated that *acqua dolce* means *fresh water*, a less used English synonym of which is *sweet water*. So in considering the last word *mare*, *sea*, which is *salt water*, *dolce* takes on a contradictory significance in which sinking in this sea or *going under* as I have it, whether or not actually drowning, is not after all a salty thing but a restorative, refreshing, sweet thing.

In support of my argument, if such is needed, for I found this after my translation was done, I quote from a letter to Pietro Giordani dated 30 April 1817—"L'Infinito" is two years later—in which Leopardi writes of Recanati, inland but no more than ten kilometres as the crow flies from what was then its coastal fishing port, now a resort: "You have been misinformed that the air of this city is salubrious. It is very changeable, damp, salty, hard on the nerves and no good at all for certain constitutions on account of its thinness."—*The Letters of Giacomo Leopardi, 1817–1837*, selected and trans. Prue Shaw (Leeds, Northern Universities, 1998). It is my understanding that what I take to be a conscious antimony has passed unnoticed in Leopardi studies, whether in English, Italian, or elsewhere.

The two most recent translations with the widest currency, by Galassi and Parks, are no less troublesome than others. Why? after so many years is a rhetorical question. In keeping with another translator, Galassi starts off on a wrong foot by deciding that the title says "Infinity". It does not. But then how much good can be said of Galassi's *Canti* (Penguin, 2010; FSG, 2012) all round. It attends to neither accuracy nor the imaginative. It is all over the place. That the complete task he set himself is heroic cannot be an excuse. Both Galassi, and Parks in a translation embedded in his introduction to *Passions* (Yale–Margellos, 2014), a rather differently voiced selected translation than the committee-translated complete Z, about which he was backhanded in *NYRB*, are stuck on *lonely*. Many see Leopardi as a lonely figure but whether he was or was not does not make a hill. Leopardi spoke of himself as *solitary*. Galassi, like almost all translators, gives the easy-to-settle-for and, as we have seen, all-important *sweet*. Parks is unspeakable: *I find pleasure drowning*. True, Leopardi talks a great deal about pleasure in Z but Z is not the poem. Two other translators are also all at sea with *pleasant* and *easeful*, while for a third, quite recent, it's, What? *a joy*. Unattributed poetry subtitles to *Il Giovane Favoloso*, a compassionate 2014 biopic, are, predictably, Galassi's.

Elsewhere, a curious translation by Jonathan Culler in his *Theory of the Lyric* (Harvard, 2015) does not recognize "stormir" as a false friend and has, improbable in the scene, "the wind / Storming through these branches".

Let the last word be Leopardi's. "Besides, sometimes the soul might desire, and actually does desire, a view that is restricted or confined in some way, as in Romantic situations. The reason is the same, a desire for the infinite, because then, instead of sight, the imagination is at work and the fantastic takes over from the real. The soul imagines what it cannot see, whatever is hidden by that tree, that hedge, that tower, and wanders in an imaginary space and pictures things in a way that would be impossible if its view could extend in all directions, because the real would exclude the imaginary."—from *Z* 171 (12–23 July 1820).

Not the last word. At last I find a place for this by Italo Calvino: "I find it very plausible that one can make the equivalent of a poem with the way one arranges trees, but I suspect that real trees are of little or no use for writing a poem about trees." and "Or that it makes no sense to expect a landscape to dictate poems to you, because a poem is made of ideas and words and syllables, whereas a landscape is composed of leaves and colours and light."—"Japan", in *Collection of Sand*, trans. M. L. McLaughlin (Penguin, 2013). Serendipitously, Xavier Kalck points to a Leopardian evocation in Louis MacNeice: "As with the hawthorn hedge, what lies beyond once more combines escape and the inescapable, 'infinite possibility' and 'a sense of eternity.'"—*Muted Strings: Louis MacNeice's* The Burning Perch (Paris, PUF–CNED, 2015). And then what is more: "From far away, peering gently and discreetly over at what is near at hand, we perceive something we would dearly love to have nearby: the unknown and yet all too intimate, familiar distance."—Robert Walser, "Watteau", in *Looking at Pictures*, trans. Susan Bernofsky (Christine Burgin / New Directions, 2015).

—

[1] "had" is an amendment to the 2016 version which reads "have".
[2] Matilde Manara adds, email, 20 January 2023: *ermo* indeed means *solitary*: not as a sort of analogy with Leopardi's soul [. . .] but as a sort of refuge from "crowded" Recanati. Plus, Leopardi seems here to be playing with registers: whereas *sempre caro* is very familiar, *ermo* should have sounded literary already at this epoch.

KADIA MOLODOWSKY

Dear Friend, Pull Out All the Stops and Help Me Get My Visa

extract translated from the Yiddish with Raphael Koenig

online in an essay by Raphael Koenig, 2023
https://www.artseverywhere.ca/series/yiddishland

I'll wind my watch again, early on the morrow
write letters, oh, you know, you know, such sorrow:
"dear friend, I'm writing you with words like these, ah
poet, pull out all the stops and help me get my visa."
then the world will know how poets rhyme
swift and shameless.
"who would answer a letter
from some stateless
minority, already that, thank god . . ."
don't laugh, my walls.
I'm quite discouraged.
[. . .]
I'll wind my watch again, early on the morrow
such hasty bitter days.
go hunt, my wild horses, shy of shays.
my coat lies ready on the chair
my gray scarf too.
open is my light valise—
"so, poet, pull out all the stops and help me get my visa please."

Transliteration of the title
"Bamit zikh liber khaver, far mir vegn a vize", in
In land fun mayn gebeyn [In the Country of My Bones]
Chicago, Shteyn, 1937

ANTHONY BARNETT

Rafael Alberti

*in Snow 7, Spring 2019
and in Like Those of an Eerie Ruin, 2019*

I do not care for embodiments of
bullfights nor do I care for ekphrasis
so why do I admire the phrases
of your poems of hereof and thereof?

El Puerto de Santa María might
be troubling to the imagination
taken for who knows what obligation
to the harbour arbour of your birthright.

Breathing in the smells of the solera
love as a child in a bodega
saca sack and Xerex Jerez sherry.

Anyway, your poems are marvellous,
the bullfight's terror dispells the grievous
benevolence the painter will foresee.

An attempt at a sonnet structured in the manner of a Rafael Alberti sonnet roughly speaking. He wrote an autobiography *La arboleda perdida* hence "arbour" in the sonnet. Alberti's family was engaged in the sherry trade, my father too

ANTHONY BARNETT ET LE CAS DES
TRADUCTIONS « ALLOPHONES »

Université de Lille
Monday, 12 December 2022

Roundtable organized by Xavier Kalck (Université de Lille), Claire Hélie (Université de Lille), Julie Loison-Charles (Université de Lille), Laetitia Sansonetti (Université Paris-Nanterre) with the participation of Anthony Barnett; Noriko Berlinguez-Kōno (Université de Lille) for the Japanese; Olivier Brossard (Université Gustave Eiffel) for the French; Anders Löjdström (Université de Lille) for the Swedish; Léandre Lucas (Université de Lille) for the Russian; Matilde Manara (Collège de France) for the Italian; and students

At the time of going to press a summary, mostly in French, of the proceedings, mostly in English, is scheduled to be posted at either https://xlingtransl.hypotheses.org or https://quaderna.org